M O O S E

For Beth —
Best ever moose!

Bill Silliker Jr.

MOOSE

Giant of the Northern Forest

BILL SILLIKER, JR.

FIREFLY BOOKS

A FIREFLY BOOK

Cataloguing in Publication Data

Silliker, Bill
  Moose: giant of the northern forest

Includes index.
ISBN 1-55209-255-0

1. Moose. I. Title.

QL737.U55S544 1998a   599.65'7   C98-930398-5

Published in Canada in 1998 by Key Porter Books Limited.

Published in the United States in 1998
by Firefly Books (U.S.) Inc.
P.O. Box 1338
Ellicott Station
Buffalo, New York, USA
14205

Design: Scott Richardson
Electronic formatting: Jean Lightfoot Peters

Printed and bound in Italy

98 99 00 01 6 5 4 3 2 1

Successful wildlife photography requires that you have respect and appreciation for your subject. It also requires persistence and much patience. And so I dedicate this book to those who taught me a bit about those things:

to Nana Silliker, whose love of nature was contagious, and who taught me to respect all wild creatures;

to Uncle Gren Redding, who first got me interested in photography and most especially in moose;

to my father-in-law, Nick Montuori, who taught me what it means to "hang in there" even when the odds are long; and

to our faithful dogs Bosley and Yoda, who waited patiently at home while many of these photographs were made.

You all go to the woods with me. I wish you were here.

C O N T E N T S

ONE

A MOOSE ENCOUNTER

An Alaskan bull peers at the camera. This bull followed the

scent of a cow for several miles across the taiga before he found her and

teamed up with her.

The bull moose tossed his head and grunted a challenge at me.

A massive bull moose, his five-foot-wide rack of hardened bone antlers gleaming in the late September sun, loomed out of the thick forest close to where the cow moose munched on willows along the far shore of the pond. The big bull curled his lips and sniffed the air before he croaked gently to her. The cow looked up and, encouraged, the bull grunted again.

How I wished I could get to their side of the pond!

It was a long shot, even for my 800mm—about 16x—of telephoto lens firepower. The moose rut, or mating season, was well under way and these two

The big bull dropped his head to display his impressive rack of antlers. Bulls sometimes do this just before they charge a rival.

Moose are actually
quite timid during
most of the year. The
exceptions are a cow
with a calf and a rut-
ting bull.

looked as if they might be about to offer a good photo opportunity with a display of rutting behavior. And so while the two moose sized each other up, I hopscotched on rocks as far out into the pond as that precarious path permitted. The one hundred feet or so gained helped. I set my tripod up in the water while balancing on a large rock and wished again that there had been time to work around the pond.

A basic rule of wildlife photography is that you take what you can get before you try to improve on it much. You don't know if you'll get a better chance, and you might miss the shot you've got. Getting around that pond, through the thick spruce and fir forest that grew down to its edge, would take time and could cost me the shot at hand. So I stayed on the rock and got ready to photograph the action.

The bull took a giant step closer to the cow and uttered a low grunt. Then the bull tossed his head to show his antlers and grunted again. I shot a few frames of the distant behavior before the cow stepped into the dark forest edge and the bull, sniffing the air, followed close behind. The two huge animals then did what often amazes those who watch moose: they disappeared into that thickest of woods without making a sound.

I decided to stay out on the rock in the pond, just in case they came out of the forest again. While waiting, I contented myself with watching a cow on the near shore.

It was all his call and he did what most moose do: he blustered and he bellowed and finally he just walked away.

They did come out of the woods again not ten minutes later. Only this time they came out of the woods directly behind me!

The bull was so interested in following his cow that at first he didn't see me. She seemed to enjoy playing it coy as she led him on. Or perhaps she wasn't on the same rutting schedule as he? Cow moose are in estrus for only a short time, while the bulls are ready and willing for over a month.

Suddenly the big bull glanced to where I crouched on the rock in the pond. His expression changed to one of pure annoyance and he turned away from his cow and sauntered toward me. As he did, he tossed his head and grunted a challenge.

This bull moose crossed the pond in search of a mate during the fall moose rut.

Bull moose in the rutting season can be the most ornery and unpredictable of animals. It's prudent to give them plenty of space or to have a climbable tree handy if for some reason you decide to approach one. But this bull had caught me out on a rock in the pond with no place to go.

You didn't need a heavy telephoto lens or tripod to get his picture then; a 180mm lens, a moderate telephoto lens that's easily hand held, worked just fine. Even with the shorter lens I could still count his teeth when he grunted yet another challenge. I knew enough about moose to know that he could mean big trouble.

He stopped some fifty feet away and lowered his long shaggy nose toward the pond to fully display his impressive rack of antlers.

They looked even more impressive through the camera lens. The bull slowly swung his antlers back and forth to make sure that I got the point before he pitched his head upward into a bugling posture that was reminiscent of his distant relative, the elk.

Then the big guy grunted another challenge. Had he mistaken me for one of his own? Moose do have rather poor eyesight. But we were so close!

I decided to talk to him. I told him that I only wanted his picture. I told him that the cow moose was all his, after all, fair was fair, he'd seen her first. I told him that he needn't worry, she was beautiful, but she wasn't my type. I couldn't think of anything else to tell him.

You just never know what a bull moose is thinking, especially during September and October.

This bull did battle with the brush along the shore before he walked past the photographer in his quest for a mate.

Maybe the sound of a human voice helped him to decide that I was not a rival. Perhaps he felt he'd won our challenge. Or did our confrontation end because his cow headed off along the shore of the pond? I'll never know. I only know how good it felt when he decided to follow her.

Even as he did, he grunted another warning to me to keep away from his cow. How could he have known that he didn't need to waste his breath?

Can a close encounter with a moose end in disaster? While it certainly can, it's not likely to happen. Many folks across the moose range in North America

have experienced a near miss with a moose, but excluding traffic accidents, the record shows that moose have actually hurt people in only a few incidents.

That's not to say that one can overlook the hazards presented by a wild animal as big and as potentially dangerous as a moose. Moose have stomped two people to death in two separate incidents in recent years in Alaska. And while much of Alaska remains as wild a place as you can find in North America today, what might surprise you is that both fatalities occurred in suburban areas.

When you consider that close to a million moose roam the northern forests—all across Canada except for Prince Edward Island, across the northern tier of the lower forty-eight United States and in most of Alaska—it says

Some bulls get so focused on the rut that they ignore much of what's going on around them. This bull walked right past a group of photographers, croaking as he went in hopes of attracting a cow to mate with.

something about their demeanor that only a handful of people have experienced dangerous encounters with these largest deer in the world. Moose are cervids, members of the deer family Cervidae, distant relations of the wapiti or North American elk, the caribou, the mule deer, and the whitetail.

All moose deserve respect for their size alone. But since most moose behave calmly and quite shyly most of the time, moose should be respected, not feared.

Henry David Thoreau, the American naturalist and philosopher, described them this way in his classic *The Maine Woods*, published in 1864: "They made me think of great frightened rabbits, with their long ears and half inquisitive half frightened looks."

An accurate description? Most moose will peer at you with a curious look on their face, often with an equal display of timidity that surprises as you contemplate their huge size. A full-grown bull of the subspecies *Alces alces americana*, the one Thoreau encountered, commonly called the Canadian moose, stands over seven feet tall at the shoulders, has about a forty-inch-long leg, is ten feet long from nose to tail, and could weigh as much as 1,400 pounds. An Alaskan moose would be even larger.

I have stood close to many bull moose of that size, even during the rut, and never felt as threatened as I did that day on the rock. Partly that's because I usually have an escape route planned.

It was all up to the moose: there was no tree to climb or even to stand behind. It was his call. And he did what moose most often do: he blustered and he bellowed and when he was satisfied he had convinced me that he was the king of that chunk of forest, he just walked away.

I treasure the photographs that he posed for and welcome the opportunity to share them and images of many other moose from across the continent with you in this book. Long live the North American moose! They truly make the northern forest a very special place.

This Alaskan bull showed no fear as he turned his back on the photographer.

TWO

MOOSE
THROUGH
THE AGES

Boreal forests with wetlands and shallow ponds make good moose habitat.

Moose arrived in North America in recent times after evolving from a similar creature that inhabited Asia only two million years ago

Would it surprise you to learn that our present-day North American moose evolved from a primitive species that inhabited Asia sometime during the Pleistocene, or most recent times, the period in the geological history of the earth that began about two million years ago? While the great glaciers of the Ice Age shrank the world's oceans, ancestors of our moose crossed on the land bridge that connected Asia and North America where the Bering Sea now separates Siberia from Alaska.

While fossil remains of moose and similar creatures indicate a presence in parts of North America at least 150,000 years ago, nobody knows exactly when the majority of the animals that we call moose spread across North America. Most researchers agree that significant moose dispersal probably came only within the last ten thousand years or so, as the last of the great glaciers retreated northward.

Other ancient moose spread westward from Asia to populate most of Europe. Fossil records show that early ancestors of the moose lived in Europe as early as two million years before the present.

Fossils of extinct mooselike creatures, including the broadheaded elk (*Alces latifrons*), found in Pleistocene deposits in Europe, and the stag-moose (*Cervalces scotti*), found in Pleistocene deposits in North America, also suggest that the evolution from the primitive ancestor of our modern-day moose has been a varied one. These two animals were apparently relatives, rather than ancestors, of our moose and evolved from an earlier common species.

The stag-moose found in North America was about the size of a present-day Alaskan moose, but with less palmated antlers that bore unique trumpet-like plates on them. Fossil remains of this animal have been found in such diverse places as Alaska, New Jersey, Illinois, Ontario, and Virginia. The species we call moose apparently replaced this stag-moose across much of its range when it became extinct sometime after the last glacier, or about ten thousand years ago.

When you look at a
moose you have to
wonder what hap-
pened to it during the
process of evolution.

While all of this may seem a long time ago, it is quite recent in the calendar of evolution. Consider that the loon, an animal as symbolic of the northern forest as the moose, has existed for some fifty million years, perhaps longer. Fossils of larger loonlike birds at least eighty million years old have been found in North America.

Doesn't it seem curious to think of the moose as a recently evolved species and a newcomer to North America? When you compare its beastly semblance with that of the graceful white-tailed deer, a distant relative that evolved in

Moose range includes tundra where moose find abundant willows and various shrubs and herbs to eat.

North America some four million years ago, don't you wonder what happened to the moose that it has such a prehistoric appearance?

It might also surprise you to learn some of the places that moose lived on the North American continent during the Pleistocene. How about Pennsylvania? Illinois? Ohio? Would you believe Oklahoma? South Carolina? Blocked from much of their present range by the great glaciers, and later by the huge glacial Lake Agassiz centered in Minnesota, early moose lived much farther south than they do today. The habitat across the balance of North America was also different then, with some southern areas more hospitable to a cold weather creature such as the moose.

Tracking the evolution of the North American moose has proven difficult for fossil hunting researchers due to the impacts of the several glaciers that scoured the surface of North America during the Pleistocene. But it seems safe to say that the movement of moose into much of the northern boreal forest that most folks consider moose country may have been an even more recent event. References in the journals left by the early white explorers and settlers have provided valuable clues for researchers.

In his comprehensive study first published in 1955, *North American Moose*, Canadian moose biologist Randolph L. Peterson reported finding no definite indication of moose among the writings of early explorers until Samuel de Champlain described such an animal in his reports of explorations begin-

ning in 1603. American naturalist Ernest Thompson Seton, in his earlier series *Lives of Game Animals*, pointed to the absence of a description of moose among the wildlife seen by Jacques Cartier on his 1535 explorations up the St. Lawrence River to what is now Montreal. Seton found the earliest clear reference to moose to be by Lescarbot, who explored "New France" in the early

This bull demonstrates why original Americans called these strange-looking deer "twig eaters."

1600s and who included a likeness of a moose on a map of Port Royal, Nova Scotia, drawn in 1609.

Historical references to moose from later in the 1600s and especially from the 1700s tell us that people did quite commonly encounter moose in parts of Maine, Manitoba, Massachusetts, New Hampshire, New York, Nova Scotia, New Brunswick, Ontario, Quebec, Vermont, and even Pennsylvania during colonial days. Much evidence indicates that moose provided an important source of food and clothing for both the original people and the new white settlers.

When explorers later ventured into other regions of North America, they also found moose: in Alaska, Alberta, and the Northwest Territories; in northern Michigan, Minnesota, and Wisconsin, and in parts of the Yukon.

It's interesting to note a lack of reports of moose from early expeditions into some places where they thrive today. Lewis and Clark trekked across Montana, Idaho, Washington, and Oregon in the early 1800s and never personally saw a moose. Expeditions to the Yellowstone region throughout the 1800s reported no moose. Early wildlife researcher George Shiras III, for whom the North American subspecies *Alces alces shirasi* is named, discovered the first known moose herd in Yellowstone National Park in the early 1900s.

Other evidence, including the oral histories of original peoples and studies by wildlife researchers of the past one hundred years, indicates that moose have adjusted their range in reaction to changes in the North American landscape wrought by a combination of human development, climatic conditions, forestry practices, and continued forest succession into new regions after the final remnants of the last glacier receded. Some researchers believe that moose

A young bull of the Canadian, or Eastern subspecies (*Alces alces americana*) enjoys a pond in early summer. Moose in the eastern portions of North America frequent ponds more than some of their western relatives do. This bull is shedding its winter coat and also growing a set of antlers.

A moose calf sleeps securely under its Canadian moose mother (*A. a. americana*) as the sun sets for another day. Canadian moose range as far west as eastern Ontario. Their coat is darker than the western subspecies.

have only expanded into some of their present western range in the last hundred years or so in a process that may still be going on.

We have also learned that man can severely impact moose through over-hunting and alteration of their habitat. Excess exploitation of moose probably

Twin moose calves of the Northwestern subspecies (*Alces alces andersoni*) who lost their mother and were rescued from the wild before they starved or were preyed upon. Moose calves across North America have a similar appearance.

began with the original people. While they are known to have had great admiration, even religious respect for wildlife, they had no system of science to understand the impacts they might be having on a species—especially one as easy to hunt as the moose. Early white settlers also encouraged their exploitation of moose. Records of seventeenth-century Jesuit missionaries and white traders document the trading of large numbers of moose hides by the Indians. Combined with the more effective weapons of the white man, such exploitation took its toll. Moose soon became scarce in many parts of their range.

During the latter half of the nineteenth century, game, market, and lumber camp hunting severely impacted remaining moose populations in Maine, New Brunswick, Nova Scotia, Quebec, and Ontario. By then moose had already disappeared from Massachusetts, Michigan, New Hampshire, New York, Pennsylvania, Wisconsin, and Vermont.

Various efforts to protect this valuable resource finally began during the late 1800s. Gradually, province by province, state by state, conservationists and naturalists worked to convince both the public and governments that moose needed protection. Once afforded some protection, moose numbers in most regions began to recover.

Changes in land management practices, such as where abandoned farmlands were allowed to return to successional forestlands and regions where cutting of mature forests led to large areas of regrowth, made a difference in the recovery of moose herds. Moose did better in such regions than in others, and those recently responsible for managing wildlife populations began to realize how little they actually knew. Serious studies of the impacts of man, predation, disease, and habitat changes began in the early 1900s and continue to this day.

In an effort to expand the range of moose, a cow and a bull from Nova Scotia were released during the 1870s on Newfoundland, where moose had not previously existed. Several more moose were introduced there in the early 1900s. Moose were also reintroduced to Cape Breton Island and the Adirondacks, where they had previously ranged but had been exterminated.

While early moose researchers had to rely mostly on personal observations, biologists today employ aids such as computers, laboratory analysis, radio collars, and helicopters as they seek to gain more knowledge about moose. Wildlife management agencies need to understand the dynamics that various impacts have on a given moose herd. Biologists have learned much about the habitats that moose prefer and where they do best, and that knowledge has helped as they attempt to manage moose herds in balance with an

A Yellowstone moose mother and her newborn calf (*Alces alces shirasi*). Adults of this subspecies are paler than the other three subspecies of North American moose.

A Yellowstone (*A. a. shirasi*) bull moose prepares for winter by leaving the mountains for the willowed lowlands near Jackson, Wyoming. The smallest of the four North American subspecies, Shiras moose range across Wyoming, Montana, Idaho, Utah, in parts of Colorado and Washington, and into southern British Columbia.

area's "carrying capacity": how many of a given species a particular habitat or range will support.

Boreal regions with willows and wetlands, shallow ponds and lakes, new-growth successional mixed hardwood and coniferous forests, or tundra and river bottoms rich with shrubs and herbs—these places constitute good moose country. Why? Because moose live where they eat.

And what do they eat? Moose browse on the leaves and twig ends of a wide variety of shrubs and trees, including willow, quaking aspen, white birch, pin cherry, red maple, balsam fir, and some spruce. They also eat fibrous forbs, such as bunchberry, the seeds of grass and sedge, bark stripped from red maple trees and aspens, and ferns and fungi. Moose even eat fallen leaves in the autumn, and lots of them. During the spring and summer months, moose that live in regions with shallow ponds with the right species of aquatic vegetation thrive on plants such as pond weed, bog rush arrowhead, yellow pond lily, and others.

Moose are ruminants. They chew their cud much the same as a domestic cow does, as they process food through a four-chambered stomach. Moose eat as much as fifty pounds a day during the summer, when vegetation is wetter and weighs more. Winter browse consumption probably averages thirty-five pounds a day. With an appetite like that, can you imagine how easily a moose

could clear your lawn of fallen maple leaves?

Some moose migrate seasonally in search of adequate food. Recent research has shown that moose, once considered to have permanent small home ranges with a radius of from two to ten miles, may actually move a considerable distance in response to seasonal changes that impact their food supply. Moose in some parts of Maine move up to flat, open mountaintops where

winds keep snow depths down and permit access to balsam fir and other browse. Moose in Wyoming do the reverse. They leave the rugged mountains of the Tetons and head for the flatland and willows around Jackson Hole. And some Alaskan moose abandon the tundra for warmer coastal regions. How far moose migrate depends upon the habitat and how well it supports them. Many moose are actually quite sedentary and live all of their days within a few miles of their birth site.

That modern moose management has been successful in much of North America is indicated by recent estimates of their numbers. A 1990–91 estimate of moose herds compiled by biologists across their range in two territories, nine provinces, and eleven states totaled a population of 976,875 moose.

Estimates of wildlife populations are done today with the help of aerial surveys and computer modeling. So it's more than a little amazing that early naturalist Ernest Thompson Seton theorized the number of moose each square mile of range might support, estimated the total North American moose range at 3,500,000 square miles, and wrote in 1927: "... at a very rough estimate, we may put the number on the whole range at a round of 1,000,000 of moose...."

Canadian jurisdictions counted the most moose in the 1990–91 survey. Moose were plentiful in Alberta, British Columbia, Newfoundland, Ontario, Quebec, Saskatchewan, and the Yukon.

In the United States, Alaska had the most moose of any state. Its estimated 155,000-strong moose herd was second only to that of British Columbia, which reported the highest count of any of the twenty-two jurisdictions with some 175,000 moose.

A cow of the Alaskan, or Yukon subspecies (*Alces alces gigas*) with a week-old calf. This cow has scars on her hide, perhaps from a fight with a predator. She stayed near this small pond for more than a week to let her youngster get strong enough to travel.

This Northwestern cow moose (*A. a. andersoni*), one of a declining population on the Agassiz National Wildlife Refuge in northern Minnesota, appears to be quite healthy. The ragged look is from the normal spring molt of her winter coat. This subspecies, which inhabits several midwestern states, appears very similar to the Canadian subspecies but is a bit smaller.

Ontario and Newfoundland also estimated well over 100,000 moose each. And while Maine ran a distant second to Alaska for United States jurisdictions, and ranked tenth overall, it reported a density of moose per square mile in some areas that was higher than any other in North America.

In recent years, moose numbers have greatly expanded in parts of their historic range where not long ago it was a novelty to see a moose: in northern New Hampshire and Vermont, as well as in several of the western United States.

Moose are also on the move. A handful of moose have taken up residence in New York's Adirondacks and in semirural areas of Connecticut!

The European and Asian descendants of primitive moose that inhabit forested areas of Europe and Asia today, including Finland, Norway, Sweden, Russia, Manchuria, Mongolia, and Siberia, are called elk: the European elk, Manchurian elk, and Siberian elk. But these are not the elk, also called wapiti, of North America. No, these European elk look like the animal that North Americans know as moose.

The name *moose* stems from the Native American Algonquian language. It means "eater of twigs," which is a pretty good description of what a moose does. Early English and some French explorers and settlers adopted the word *moose*.

The Basque French explorers called the large deerlike animals that they

saw *orenac,* which is Basque for deer. *Orenac* then evolved to *orignac* to finally become the French Canadian *l'orignal* that survives today.

The closest relatives of moose, the European elk, exist in great numbers today in some parts of the Old World, as evidenced by the results reported for the 1982–83 "moose" hunt in Sweden, when nearly 180,000 European elk (*Alces alces alces*) were harvested to control a burgeoning population. Some 1 million European elk—or moose—have been harvested in Sweden alone from 1980 to 1995. Sweden may hold a claim to the highest density of moose in the world.

The evolution of the moose—*l'orignal*—elk—is a complicated one. While scientists are still sorting out the details and as new discoveries fill in the gaps, most researchers agree that the four subspecies alive today in North America— the Alaskan or Yukon moose; the Canadian or Eastern moose; the Northwestern moose; and the Yellowstone or Shiras moose—are close relatives of the three subspecies of elk that survive in Europe and Asia.

Let's take a closer look at the North American animal called the moose.

A prime Alaskan bull (*A. a. gigas*) during the rut. Alaskan moose are the largest in the world and can weigh as much as 1,800 pounds.

THREE

MOOSE OF ALL AGES

A Maine moose calf quickly learns about snow and cold when it

meets its first winter.

A yearling bull, ragged from the shedding of his winter coat of guard hairs, searches for the mother that abandoned him.

The cow moose emerged from the black spruce forest and followed a well-worn trail through the bog laurel and the rhodora that was in full bloom along the shore. She stopped at the water's edge to look out across the pond for a moment, then turned and peered back into the woods. What was she looking at?

The answer came within a minute, when a smaller moose stepped out of the woods behind her. Twin knobs on its head described it as a male. Both its smaller size and the fact that its antler growth was so insignificant by mid-May revealed it to be a yearling.

A mother moose chases away her yearling while her new calf waits on shore.

The younger moose appeared uncertain of itself as it approached the cow. The cow held her head higher and turned to face the yearling. The hair on the nape of her neck flared. Her ears dropped back, flat on her head.

The younger moose looked away, obviously afraid to make eye contact. He grunted, a soft, plaintive sound.

The cow held her head even higher. Her threatening posture was now unmistakable. But the message it conveyed was apparently one that the younger moose didn't want to receive. He grunted again and took a few steps closer.

He pushed his luck when he edged up beside the angry cow. She lashed out at him with a foreleg. Her quick kick just missed the yearling as he jumped backward and spun in a rapid turn away from her. He ran back to the treeline before he stopped to look back at her and grunt once more. What a sad sight he made!

But the cow moose no longer showed an interest in him. She walked into the shallow pond, and when the water reached her chest, she began to swim.

She swam across the pond without looking back. It was only after she had exited the pond on the far shore that she finally cast a sidelong glance back toward her pitiful yearling. Satisfied that he would stay where he was, she shook the excess water from her coat before she disappeared into the woods.

The bewildered yearling watched the spot where his mother had vanished. What had he done to anger her so? Why would she not let him near her today?

Moose mothers nuzzle their youngsters to help establish a maternal bond. How many moose are in the photograph? If you said three immediately, you have a good eye.

These moose calves were found orphaned by researchers exploring the causes of a significant decline in the moose population at and around the Agassiz National Wildlife Refuge in Minnesota.

What should he do now? He decided to wait for her to return.

The yearling waited for a long time, but his mother didn't come out of the woods again. After a while he entered the dark forest and rambled up the trail away from the pond, a trail he'd never traveled alone before. And as he did, he wondered once again why his mother had abandoned him.

Variations of the drama described above take place every May all across moose country. Moose mothers suddenly turn on the offspring that they have protected and guided throughout the past year and signal them to stop following. The yearlings don't understand and they attempt to tag along at a distance. When they try to get closer, the cow moose postures and tells them with body language, sometimes audibly, to get away. If a yearling persists, its mother will chase it off. She may even kick it.

While it's risky to attribute humanlike "feelings" to any animal, I've watched enough moose in these situations to be comfortable describing a yearling's thoughts as ones of bewilderment. Moose may not think in the same way that humans do, but they often demonstrate behaviors that indicate that they have distinct wants and desires. The desire of a yearling moose to maintain its relationship with its mother may be one of the most clearly displayed non-mating-related behaviors in nature. The antagonism of a mother moose as she attempts to discourage a persistent yearling appears to be just as deeply "felt." She demonstrates those feelings with threats and aggressive action.

A moose calf forms a strong bond with its mother, one that begins at birth and strengthens as the calf follows its mother throughout its first year. The calf learns from its mother everything that it needs to know to survive in the world. And so the idea that Mother suddenly doesn't want it near her anymore devastates the yearling moose. But sooner or later, every yearling gets the message.

Are mother moose indifferent to their yearlings? Not really. They're just following the cycle of nature. That cycle requires that a pregnant moose cow must shake herself free of her yearling before the end of May. She will soon need to focus all of her attention on the difficult task of raising the next generation.

Moose give birth from late May

into early June after a gestation period of some 240 days. Studies indicate that moose conform to a remarkably similar birth schedule all across their North American range. They need to: at about three feet long and three feet tall, a newborn moose has a lot of surface area in relation to its body weight, which averages twenty-five to thirty pounds. A moose calf requires a good deal of energy just to keep warm due to its surface area to body mass ratio. Born too soon into the cold spring of the northern forest and it could easily freeze to death. Born too late and it cannot grow enough body mass to prepare for the inevitable cold of the approaching winter.

Moose cows seek security and solitude prior to giving birth. Some prefer the relative safety offered by islands or peninsulas in ponds, lakes, and rivers. Others find the seclusion of densely forested patches adequate. Research has shown that refuge, food, and the ready availability of water seem to influence a cow moose's decision as to the adequacy of a birth site.

Moose probably give birth to twins from about one third to perhaps one half of the time. One study in Algonquin Provincial Park in Ontario showed a wide fluctuation in cows seen with twins from year to year, with as few as 7 percent to as many as 80 percent of the cows having twins over a ten-year period. Some cows even give birth to triplets, but this is quite rare. And at least one case of quadruplets has been documented!

The quality and quantity of nourishment during the long winter of a cow's

Moose mothers defend their youngsters and can be dangerous to those who approach too closely.

A calf hides behind its mother, who maintains her protective role. By fall a moose calf looks much more like its mother.

pregnancy directly affects her productivity from year to year. The food supply that a given habitat provides also impacts upon the survivability of the newborn calves in all such multiple births.

The cow gives birth lying down after about an hour of labor. She will immediately nuzzle and lick her offspring. This helps the cow to establish a maternal bond with her calf. Some researchers believe that such nuzzling also helps stimulate bodily processes in a newborn moose calf that are vital for its survival. Whatever the case, the process of bonding with the mother begins at birth.

Surprisingly enough, a new moose doesn't look much like its mother. Its coat is a reddish brown, more the color of a golden retriever than the dark brown or black of an adult moose. Its eyes are circled in black. And its nose is shorter in relation to its face than that of the adult moose. Still, there's no mistaking the offspring of a moose.

A moose calf receives its first milk from its mother soon after birth while both remain lying down. Within a few days, a calf can easily reach its standing mother as she nurses it.

For its first several days, a calf moves about very little and on rather wobbly legs. But within a week, it can easily outrun a human.

Cow moose stay within a hundred feet of the birth site for the first several days. A cow will linger close to the birth site for a week, perhaps longer, unless forced to leave by a predator. Depending on her home range—the liv-

The typical moose "family" is a sight you'll only see during a few short weeks in the fall.

A moose calf will stay close to its mother throughout the winter. Her guidance can make a difference in its survival during this most difficult season of the year.

These Wyoming moose (Alces alces shirasi) gathered at a feeding site.

OPPOSITE PAGE: Sometimes a yearling moose will even follow along with a human as it seeks companionship.

ing space that an animal customarily uses—she may wander farther in search of food after the first week. When moose mothers do leave the birth area, they bring their babies with them. The young moose will learn to swim when only a week old where water is an important part of the home range.

Unlike most other members of the deer family—the mule deer, elk, and whitetail—moose are not hiders of their babies. While they sometimes will use concealment, moose rely mostly on defending their offspring. If they can't avoid and evade danger, they will stand and fight. Mother moose are in fact among the most protective in nature, ranking with the grizzly, or brown bear, as willing defenders of their offspring.

Those who doubt that should consider the response of Tim Williams, a net gunner or "shooter" for Helicopter Wildlife Management, when asked what

was the most dangerous species he'd encountered in making his living jumping from a hovering helicopter to capture live wildlife. I met Tim in May 1996 at the Agassiz National Wildlife Refuge in northwestern Minnesota, when Helicopter Wildlife Management was assisting in a project to research the causes of a severe decline in the moose population of the area. Tim was hand-capturing recently born moose without a net while the pilot maneuvered the helicopter near ground level to keep their mothers at bay. They would then take the moose calf and land the helicopter at a safe site nearby where they'd quickly weigh it, take a blood sample, and radio-tag the calf so that researchers could later track it. Afterward, they would return the calf to its frantic mother.

Tim included elk, black bear, a variety of deer species, and moose among the wildlife he'd handled. And his answer as to which of those species is the most dangerous? Tim said mother moose without hesitation. When asked why, he replied: "Because they have an attitude. All they want to do is kill you."

It's worth noting Tim's words when you hike in moose country from late spring through the summer, and with some moose cows, right through the winter. Take care if you encounter a cow with a calf: your interference could result in the calf getting separated from its mother, which in predator country can prove fatal. Or the calf could get hurt running away. That's not to mention the need to consider your own safety. Beware of too close an approach to any moose calf.

To pursue wildlife photography, I either hide from a mother moose or allow her to set a distance that she feels comfortable with. If you're patient, some will approach quite close to you after they feel comfortable with your presence.

A moose calf gains weight rapidly, as much as two pounds per day in its first month and some three to five pounds per day in its next several months. It begins to browse on leaves and twigs after several weeks, but suckles milk until weaned at about five months of age.

By late summer, a calf changes its coat color to a dark brown and begins to

A persistent yearling follows its mother across a pond.

This two-week-old Alaskan calf got separated from its mother somehow and was last seen wandering across the taiga bleating for her to come to it. It would surely attract a predator with its calling unless its mother found it first.

grow the longer nose of an adult moose. By its first fall it will look like a smaller version of its mother, and could weigh several hundred pounds. The calf stays close by its mother even during the rut, or moose mating season, in September and October. This is the only time that you're likely to see a "moose family" together. That image is deceptive: bull moose show no interest in their offspring at any time of the year.

Sometimes a calf might get separated from its mother when she joins up with a bull during the rut, but only by a short distance and only for a short time. A moose calf needs its mother to lead it during the toughest time of the year for all creatures of the northern forest, the winter. Snow depth can restrict feeding, and a juvenile moose may not know where to go to find a more accessible or plentiful food supply. A moose calf without a mother would also likely be dominated by adult moose, especially cows with calves, who might prevent it from getting adequate nourishment to survive. And so a moose calf sticks with its mother right through the winter.

Despite the care and protection that mother moose provide for their youngsters, some calves succumb to a variety of causes that include predation, accidents, disease, drowning, and malnutrition. Depending on where a moose calf lives, threats to it vary, and its chances for survival will differ greatly. But if a moose calf doesn't survive to become a yearling, it's not because its mother didn't care enough.

That's why a yearling is so devastated when its mother chases it off come spring. Unless the yearling's mother is not pregnant, it must learn to fend for itself by its first birthday. The occasional lucky yearling that does get to stay with its mother has only a short reprieve. Either its mother or a rutting bull will run it off as a sexual rival when the fall mating season commences.

What becomes of the yearlings after their mothers chase them away? Some shadow their mother at a safe distance for days, sometimes even for weeks. Some wander the woods in search of a place to fit into the world again. Those lucky enough to have a sibling stay together through summer and fall and often into the winter. Yearlings who have no brother or sister may attempt to accompany another

This Minnesota calf was luckier; after it was momentarily in the custody of a U.S. Fish and Wildlife Service researcher, it was released back to its mother.

yearling or perhaps even a more adult moose. While some bulls will tolerate a follower for a while, a cow with a calf will not.

One June day in the beginning of my moose photography pursuits, my wife accompanied me for a trip to a moose pond that was a two-hour automobile ride and a fifteen-minute hike away. The sun comes up early in June, and the moose show up at this pond shortly afterward. The photographer who wants good targets in the best light has to get there early as well. But getting out of the house early is not exactly my wife's specialty, especially when early means 4:00 A.M.

We were nearly an hour late leaving the house and I was chafing. Maryellen was a real sport, though, and as we drove the miles, she told me to just leave her when we got to the trailhead. She said she'd catch up with me at the pond. She knew that I was in a rush to find a moose.

Leave her I did, or so I thought. I strapped my pack on my back and slung the tripod on my shoulder and hustled off into the woods. I'd gotten well down the trail when I first heard her call: "Bill. Wait. Wait up."

She didn't sound hurt and she didn't sound scared, so what does she want when I'm trying to get to the moose before they all head off to chew their cuds? These were just a few of the husbandly thoughts that ran through my head as I looked back for the first time.

She called again: "Wait, you fool. You're in such a hurry to see a moose.

A curious yearling stares at its own shadow on a rock.

Wait and he'll walk right past you."

I waited until I saw her and her new friend, a moose with two small bumps on his head. I'd been reading about moose and knew him to be a yearling. He followed Maryellen on the trail, not twenty feet behind her.

When Maryellen stopped, the moose stopped too. When she spotted me and started forward again, the moose tramped along behind her.

When she got a hundred feet away she said: "See? He's been following me since the parking lot. And you're rushing off to the pond."

I decided against reminding her that she'd told me to go on ahead. Instead, I suggested: "Come up here. See if he'll keep following you."

Maryellen walked ahead. Her moose friend followed. When she stopped beside me, the moose stopped too and watched us from his safe distance of twenty feet back.

"Looks like a yearling. Probably thrown out by his mom a few weeks ago," I told her with my new knowledge of moose as I pulled out a camera.

"Poor baby. He's been following me all the way from the parking lot. I think he likes me."

"Well, we can't take him home."

"I know that. Could you imagine feeding him?"

Sometimes a yearling moose will even attach itself to a human as it desperately seeks a companion to take the place of its mother, and people have taken in moose as pets. In *Lives of Game Animals*, Ernest Thompson Seton described a moose that liked to come into the kitchen of a farmhouse to escape the flies. It would sprawl on the floor and wouldn't leave, not even when the woman of the house smacked it with a broom. The farmer finally traded it for a horse.

Others report some success in the domestication of moose. The European moose have served as pack, draft, and riding animals in Sweden and Russia. Moose reportedly cannot work much during warm weather, though.

Most accounts from North America suggest that moose, while quite tame and willing as young animals, become stubborn and willful as they mature. They can present quite a hazard when they do exert a mind of

Some bulls travel

together during the

summer at Denali

National Park in

Alaska.

their own. Adult moose can kick out with a forty-inch-long leg. Even a playful kick could be dangerous.

Because moose probably don't make very good subjects for domestication, they are best left in their natural environment—even a downhearted yearling.

The springtime of confusion as yearling moose figure out their place in the world without the guidance of mother can also lead to danger: some wander onto busy highways, others may be careless about predators. But most survive, and research indicates that a moose that lives to be a year old has a good likelihood of living for many years.

Moose grow in height and length for about two years. They add weight and bulk for several more years, and could be considered in their prime from about five to ten years of age.

It's risky to judge the age of a bull moose by his antlers. Biologists have developed a way to determine the age of a moose by counting the growth layers in the cementum of a tooth, much the same as counting the rings on a tree. Records show that a moose can live twenty years or more.

Oddly enough, moose are not gregarious animals once they mature into adults on most of their North American range. The mother and calf bond that ceases when the calf reaches its first birthday is the only strong social relationship between moose outside of the brief interludes that occur during the rut.

In parts of their range where ponds provide a significant summer food source, you may see as many as a dozen moose feeding together and assume that they gather at such places. But careful observation will tell you that most of these moose came to the pond to feed separately, except for the cow and calf combinations.

Moose do occasionally "yard," or collect together at winter feeding sites, if snow depth limits movement. As tall an animal as a moose has a distinct advantage in winter, however, and moose aren't hindered by snow until it reaches chest height, unless it is crusty snow. Some moose yard together on the tops of mountains where the wind keeps the snow depths down. Others collect in wooded valleys and on the edge of clearcuts and burnt areas where new forest growth provides an abundant food supply that the moose can

reach without much movement. Moose in Wyoming congregate on the willowed lowlands near Jackson Hole during winter. But these gatherings apparently occur as moose search out food, not companionship.

Exceptions to the solitary existence led by most adult moose have been noted, particularly in Alaska. Some adult moose gather in small herds as the fall mating season approaches. At Denali National Park, each fall the cow moose without calves collect in herds of a dozen or more on the taiga, or tundralike terrain that is sparsely forested by stunted-growth spruce. Researchers believe that these associations may have something to do with the increased visibility for moose in such habitats as compared to the more densely forested regions that most moose inhabit. It may also have something to do with the predation rate at Denali: some 90 percent of the moose calves fall victim to bears and wolves there, and lone cows will unite in small herds while a cow that has a calf in tow will not.

Some of the adult bulls at Denali also mingle, but in smaller groups. Bulls often travel together in small groups of three or four as they feed during the summer.

By the time the mating season gets fully under way in September, the more dominant bulls will break away from such groups. No longer are the big bulls friends, if they ever were. It's time for the most exciting season of the moose: the rut.

This mature moose cow has grown a thick coat of guard hairs to protect her from the cold of winter. A healthy moose could live twenty years or more.

FOUR

THE MOOSE
RUT

A bull feeds in a pond after the rut as the first hint of winter streaks the air. Bulls stop feeding completely during the peak of the rut and must replenish their fat reserves quickly before the coming winter.

While some bulls develop tremendous antlers by the fall mating season, they all start each year without anything but pedicels, basal attachments for the antlers just forward of the ears.

Bull moose grow their antlers from scratch every year. As impressive a sight as the rack that some bulls cart around on their heads becomes by autumn, they all start the previous winter when two small knots of soft tissue form on what are called pedicels on the bull's head. The antlers grow and take shape beneath this blood vessel–laden tissue, appropriately named for the velvet that it resembles. Moose don't need their antlers during the winter. In fact, moose go through all the work of growing the impressive racks that trophy hunters prize for one reason only: the rut.

Moose seem to take care to avoid impacts to their developing antlers; the velvet is apparently tender. The antlers progressively calcify beneath the velvet to become the hardened bone that bulls display in the fall. The velvet dries up

The pedicels show clearly on this bull that has recently shed his antlers.

Bull moose in velvet avoid hitting their rapidly growing antlers, which could be damaged and deformed and which apparently are sensitive at the velvet stage.

A bull cleans his rack of the no longer needed, dried-up velvet. Despite the bloody appearance of the antlers, moose apparently feel no pain now that they have become hardened bone.

and peels away when it no longer serves a purpose.

The bumps of the yearling become short spikes by the fall. Palmated antlers probably develop at three years of age. As a bull matures, he commonly grows more imposing antlers each year until he reaches prime age. While the more mature bulls generally grow the better antlers, nutrition, health, and hereditary factors also play a role in determining the size of a bull moose's rack.

When you consider that a moose rack from an Alaskan bull registered with the Boone and Crockett Club big game records weighed seventy-seven pounds, and that another rack measured in excess of eighty-one inches of spread, it's hard to believe that a moose could grow such massive antlers in a matter of months!

A sparring match early in the rut. Such contests do not have the intensity of the battles that occur later in the rut, and may serve as tests to identify bulls to be avoided.

While flehmen, the curling of the upper lip to enhance the ability to evaluate scent, is most often done by rutting bulls as they check the odor of urine to determine the estrus status of a female, research has shown that all moose perform the behavior.

One mid-August day at Denali National Park I asked U.S. Forest Service moose researcher Victor Van Ballenberghe when the bulls might be likely to clean the velvet from their antlers. I was hoping to photograph one engaged in this activity on the open terrain of Denali since it's difficult to catch a moose peeling velvet in the dense forests that comprise much of their range in the East. I had to go home at the end of the month and I hoped that Vic would say "late August." But I feared his answer would be "early September."

Vic's reply amazed me.

"August twenty-fifth," he said without reflection.

"August twenty-fifth?"

Perhaps the incredulity showed on my face. It must have been clear in my voice. Vic smiled and said: "I've been studying them here for fifteen years. It's usually August twenty-fifth, give or take a day."

The bull in the photograph on page 78 cleaned his rack on August 26. While he obviously couldn't read Vic's research, he demonstrates how moose live in sync with a natural calendar.

The work of other researchers shows that to be remarkably true all across the moose range of North America. It seems that moose hormones and biological processes respond to exposure to sunlight, in what biologists call *photoperiodism*.

Moose carry on a variety of fascinating behaviors during their quest to continue the species. Those behaviors begin with the first phase of the moose rut, which commences on August 25.

First, the dried-up velvet peels away to reveal the now solid bone antlers beneath. Some velvet might cling to a bull's antlers and even hang over his face, obscuring his view. And so bulls scrape the no longer needed velvet

Bulls dig wallows throughout the rut. A cow moose in estrus will force a bull aside to get a turn in the urine-scented mud.

against trees and shrubs in an effort to remove it. Some eat the hanging shreds that they can reach or that lodge in tree branches. While the racks of many bulls may look like a bloody mess at this time, their antlers are no longer sensitive, as they were earlier in the year when the velvet pulsed with life.

The dominant bulls, the mature, hardy ones who take charge as the rut ensues, generally finish cleaning their racks first. By September 10 all the bulls should be done clearing their racks. Their hardened antlers now serve the two purposes nature had planned for them all along: to signal to cow moose that a bull may be a good choice for a mate and to defend against the other bulls for her sexual favors.

Once a bull clears his rack he may duel with another in a sparring match. Such shoving contests may look impressive, but they pale compared to the real thing, the fights and sometimes violent antler clashes that bulls will engage in as the true rut commences a few weeks later. These early sparring contests may serve to help the bulls sort out who among them are the strongest so that if they should meet later, they might choose to avoid conflict.

Bull moose dig wallows with their antlers and their front hooves as they attempt to attract a cooperative cow during the rut. A moose wallow is just what it sounds: a pit dug in the ground in which moose throw themselves and wallow around to coat their bodies with the pungent odor of urine that the bulls mark their wallows with. You can often smell moose wallows before you

A bull thrashes the woods to signal his dominance and desire to mate.

see them when hiking in moose country, especially during the peak of the rut. A bull sometimes also smacks the wet pit with a front hoof to splash himself with the muddy aphrodisiac.

Cow moose hop into the wallow pits too, often shoving a bull aside in their haste to partake of this strongly scented mud. They will also challenge other cows who attempt to use a wallow. Cows threaten other moose with a head-held-high stance and a glassy-eyed stare. They'll also strike out at a rival with a front hoof to dislodge her from the pit.

Bull moose of all ages dig wallows, apparently wherever the urge moves them, throughout the entire rut.

Both sexes rely heavily on scent to communicate sexual messages of readiness. A bull does a lip curl by raising his head and sniffing the air while retracting his upper lip in a behavior that is called *flehmen*. Bulls and cows both sniff each other's muzzles and moose urine on the ground. A bull may also sniff at a cow's genitals to detect if she is in estrus.

Moose also vocalize to communicate their desires. Bulls croak or grunt, making low-pitched sounds that rise in intensity and volume as the bull gets more excited or if he is challenging a rival. Submissive bulls often make a whining sound.

A cow may wail and moan, particularly when a bull comes close to her. And some cows who are ready to mate may moan to attract a nearby bull.

Bull moose of equal size and strength will sometimes battle with their antlers as they jostle with a rival in an attempt to gore him.

The challenger had a smaller rack of antlers but he made up the difference in determination and courage.

The bigger bull out-maneuvered the challenger, who spun around to avoid a possible goring.

Undeterred, the challenger engaged the bigger bull again and shoved with all of his might.

The second phase of the rut commences on September 11 and runs to September 25. Bulls now actively pursue cows and will defend a cow or even a group of cows. But while bull moose may travel with and defend more than one cow against other bulls, they do not control the cows as their relatives the elk, or wapiti, do. Bull elk gather a harem and will prevent a cow from leaving the group during the rut. Almost completely hormone driven now, the dominant bulls actually stop eating for the next few weeks as they continuously wander the north woods, grunting to attract a mate. Many bulls greatly

After a half hour of fighting, the two bulls finally called a truce. The bigger bull left the pond to the challenger shortly after this photograph was made.

expand their home range during the rut as they cruise the woods looking for a mate.

Bulls will defend their territory if they discover an intruder during this phase of the rut. Any less dominant bull that dares to enter their domain does so at his own risk. Bull moose have been known to chase people out of their mating area, too.

Most bulls will court a single cow. And they will fight now, perhaps even

This bull broke an antler during a fight for the mating rights to a cow. The power of a bull moose is one of the major forces to behold in the animal world.

OPPOSITE PAGE: No longer needed, the antlers become a liability during the winter. Dominant bulls usually shed their antlers first, often as early as late November. Most bulls shed from December to February.

to the death, with any bull that challenges them for her company. While some moose may congregate in groups, like the moose at Denali described in the previous chapter, bull moose do not gather harems as some species, do during the rut.

Bull moose meetings don't often end in a major battle. That's partly because a lesser bull may avoid conflict, since he knows who is the more powerful from a sparring match earlier in the rut. It's also because the smaller bulls identify the more dominant bulls during the antler displays that bull moose make to each other when they meet during the months of September and October. They toss their racks and threaten each other, flaunting what they've got to fight with—just as the bull in the first chapter did while I stood out on that rock in the pond. If an intruder doesn't back away, the dominant bull will grunt a challenge and may drop his head to fully display his antlers and make his warning clear before he charges—just as my friend did.

Bulls will also thrash the bushes and bang their antlers against trees to taunt their rivals, to work off aggression, and perhaps to work up courage. They also use tree raking to telegraph their presence to the willing cows within hearing distance.

Lesser bulls usually get the message and back off when they see that they're outgunned. But a bull of equal size and strength who sports a healthy rack himself may well stand and fight.

An Alaskan bull cruising the taiga in search of a cow as the rut proceeds toward mid-September.

The rut begins August 25, when the bulls shed their velvet. This bull, photographed in early September, has remnants of velvet hanging from his rack.

Bull moose that do battle often approach each other slowly and stiffly. They cast their antlers side to side as they glare at their rival with bloodshot eyes and grunt threats at him. They may engage their antlers in a sharp clash or they might move cautiously and assume a stance that allows them to most effectively shove their opponent.

Some may charge each other and hit head-on in a violent crash. Bulls have actually hit so hard that their antlers spread apart at the impact, then locked

A bull follows a cow across the pond in hopes that she will be receptive to his advances.

together as the antlers contracted after the collision. Moose entangled this way have died a lingering death of starvation.

Other battles may end with scarred and even broken antlers. Bulls can even pierce holes in the racks of their rivals with the force that they exert.

Antler tines driven home by a charging bull moose can also do serious damage to another bull's head or body. Bulls often attempt to gore a rival with their antlers as he spins to run away when he's outmaneuvered. The hides of most mature bull moose show many scars from punctures by antler tines. And occasionally, a goring proves fatal to the recipient.

The power of a dominant rutting bull moose is one of the major forces to behold in the animal world. His antlers truly mark him as the king of the northern forest.

Whether they realize it or not, cow moose react to the visual stimuli of a bull's antlers, but in a different way. The rack of a dominant bull moose apparently signals to a cow that this bull can provide excellent genes for their offspring. Dominant cows will chase off other cows when they team up with a prime bull.

The third phase of the rut starts when the cows reach estrus and are now willing to mate with the bulls. The peak of the rut begins on September 26 and runs to about October 10. Most of the mating actually occurs during these few weeks.

A Canadian moose grunts a mating call while checking for scent in the air during the peak of the rut.

The dominant bulls mate first during the last week of September. The less prime animals may get to mate if there are sufficient cows in a region; otherwise, they will be prevented from mating by the more aggressive dominant bulls. Lesser bulls hanging around the edge of a rutting group in the regions where such behaviors occur sometimes succeed in mating with one of the cows if the dominant bull is distracted.

The first female estrus period peaks on about October 1. Cows that do not mate during the peak of the rut will reach estrus again in mid October, and may do so again as late as early November. While this gives some of the lesser bulls and even the youngsters a chance to mate, the real moose rut winds down after October 10.

Why are moose so regular in their mating schedule? Because in order to deliver healthy offspring at the most optimum time of the year for their survival, the required gestation period for that offspring must commence on schedule.

After the rut, nature's clock ticks away progressively shorter days as winter approaches. The bulls, some of whom have lost hundreds of pounds during the rut, need to recoup their fat supply and to store energy if they are to survive the harsh weather sure to come. Bulls will sometimes eat throughout the day in late October and November.

And as the snows deepen, a bull will drop his no longer needed antlers one day to lighten his load so that he has a better chance to get through the winter. Rodents often take advantage of the protein stored in dropped antlers as the cycle of life in the north woods continues.

A Yellowstone bull takes a break from a morning of feeding to rest on the open flats near Jackson, Wyoming, as winter closes in.

FIVE

MOOSE ABILITIES, BEHAVIORS, AND CONCERNS

Moose make the northern forest a special place.

These moose calves jumped to their feet when their mother grunted that she was ready to nurse them. She had earlier used a different grunt to tell them to wait until she had chewed her cud.

Moose behave in direct response to their perception of the world around them. Their senses tell them what is happening. Their instincts, experience, and the training they received from their mother guide them in how to react.

Moose will protect themselves, usually quite successfully, from the concerns that they can detect. It's the things that they aren't aware of that cause them the most trouble.

Let's explore the five senses first. Moose have an acute sense of smell and excellent hearing. Their eyesight, adequate for most needs, doesn't compare to either of these other two senses. Moose probably also have a well-developed sense of taste and may even have a good sense of touch.

Among other things, moose use their sense of smell to detect the presence of danger, to identify each other, and to determine the sexual readiness of possible mates. Mother moose improve the bond with their offspring with the help of their sense of smell.

Moose use their excellent hearing to identify possible sources of danger and to detect the approach of other moose. Since moose rely on a combination of their keen senses of smell and hearing to alert them to possible danger, they may avoid open areas on windy days when the scent of predators is blown away and the crackling of colliding tree limbs in the nearby forest makes it difficult to hear.

They also use their hearing to receive communication from other moose.

Moose sometimes crave sodium in their diet and may find it in road treatments.

Moose talk to each other with several different grunts, moans, and wail sounds. Grunts made by cows tell calves to wait, come, or follow, or indicate that the cow is ready to nurse. The calves seem to understand exactly what is being said by their mothers and respond accordingly. Moose calves in turn bawl with an almost human sound when frightened or if they want their mother to tend to them.

Low-pitched grunts and croaks made by the bulls during the rut signal that they are in the area. Their grunts rise in volume and intensity if they

A moose can feed underwater for minutes before bursting to the surface for a breath.

become excited or sexually aroused. Cows often respond with wails and moans that communicate that they would be receptive to a male's sexual advances.

Moose can run a great distance in a very short time.

That moose don't see very well becomes apparent if you approach a moose as it feeds in a pond. You can often get to within one hundred feet of a moose if you approach from downwind so that it can't detect you by scent, move only while the moose has its head under water, and stop and stand quietly when it lifts its head, so that it cannot detect any movement or hear you.

Moose do detect movement quite readily. They also see fairly capably in the dark, as they have reflective tissue behind their retinas that acts as a light collector. Their eyes don't reflect car headlights as well as those of their whitetail relatives do, however, probably because moose stand so tall above the direct beam of the lights.

It is probable that moose have a well-developed sense of taste. Because moose feed heavily at ponds during the spring and early summer but cease most of this activity during the hottest time of the year, some researchers have speculated that the aquatic vegetation somehow sours to their taste with the seasonal changes. That may be true, because in some regions moose return to feed in ponds during the cooler fall weather.

Moose also enjoy the taste of salts that they find in road treatments and at natural mineral licks. Some moose plunk themselves prostrate on a road to lick salt off its surface in the winter or where calcium has been applied to keep dust

A calf learns to swim
when only days old.
Moose are excellent
swimmers.

down on gravel roads in the summer. They also find sodium in the vegetation along the side of the road or at licks where water runoff sometimes forms muddy spots. They seem to crave sodium most during winter, spring, and early summer. The search for salt in their diet often makes moose a road hazard.

They also get sodium from the aquatic vegetation that they search out on the bottom of shallow ponds and lakes in summer. Watch a moose poke around the bottom of a pond with its feet for a while and you begin to appreciate that they can somehow feel the aquatic vegetation with their toes. Moose often seem to know right where to go without looking to find a good spot to feed on vegetation growing underwater.

Moose often submerge completely in a pond as they feed. They are able to hold their breath for a long time: entire minutes pass while they chew on food at the bottom of a pond.

Moose can swim quite well, at least five miles per hour. They have been recorded swimming distances as long as nine miles. And it doesn't matter where. Some friends once called excitedly to alert me that a bull moose was swimming in the Atlantic Ocean in front of their house on the beach in Scarborough, Maine! I envisioned a classic image of a moose with a lighthouse in the background, but by the time I could get there, the moose had left the ocean for the cover of a nearby wetland.

Their long legs can carry them at speeds of up to thirty-five miles per hour

on land, according to several reliable accounts. Moose don't often run at full speed, however, but rely more on what might be called a trot when they are in a hurry.

A mother moose and her unruly calf display moose body language as she disciplines the calf.

If you should encounter a moose in the road, it's best not to run it ahead of your vehicle. Moose can develop blood clots in their lungs or could hurt themselves in a fall.

You may have to wait awhile for a moose to yield the road, as sometimes they can be quite stubborn. Perhaps that's why some people think that they're not very smart; I'm more inclined to believe that moose don't perceive an automobile or a small truck as a threat, perhaps because they tower over the top of such vehicles. Watch a moose respond to the approach of a honking logging truck sometime before you conclude that they're too stupid to get out of the way.

Their long legs make them lethal objects in collisions with small vehicles, as the massive bulk of their bodies comes flying at the windshield level or crashes onto the roof. Many moose die each year from traffic accidents, and people do too. Safe driving in moose country requires constant alertness and slowing down, especially when moose are apt to be on or near the road in search of salt or at known moose crossing areas.

Those long legs allow them to step right over fallen trees and rocks and stumps that slow other animals down. Moose can outlast pursuing predators

This cow is shedding her winter coat. But isn't she beautiful anyway?

by the ease with which they travel through the woods, while the predators deplete their energy as they jump over or maneuver around such obstacles.

Moose can slog through swamps and bogs with little apparent effort. Their feet have four toes: two large front toes that leave a track spanning some six inches long by about four-and-a-half inches wide, and two smaller dewclaws that are higher up on the rear of their leg and sometimes show in tracks, extending the print left by an adult moose to perhaps ten inches long. The spread of such feet permits moose to get good footing on hard, soft, and even mushy surfaces.

Sometimes overconfident moose die in bogs, as they get trapped in pond-like openings that attract them to feed and then find that there is no firm support to get out on the floating matted plant life that forms the surface of such bogs. An occasional moose also drowns from falling through thin ice.

Their long legs provide moose with weapons that they use quite effectively against predators, sometimes on other moose, and occasionally against humans who get too close. They'll lash out with a front leg or kick with their hind legs. Given the chance, they'll stomp a wolf or a bear to death.

Moose react to most threats with a "fight or flight" response. The distance at which a moose might react by either fleeing or fighting a perceived threat depends partly on the moose and the time of year, with mother moose in early

A rutting bull peers out from behind a tree to take a look at something it heard in the woods. Moose don't see see very well but have excellent hearing.

summer being the most prone to fight-or-flight behavior; the response is based partly on the moose's previous experience with such a threat and partly on its concept of feeling cornered. While one might think that a moose has many paths by which to leave an encounter, the moose may want to go the way that's blocked. Such a moose could charge to get through.

In close encounters, moose often display their intent with vocalizations, including variations on the grunts and moans described earlier, and with a variety of body language. Cows seem to most often use the "head held high stance" to threaten an opponent, be it another moose or a predator. Moose also display with their manes, as the hair on the back of their necks bristles and flares. They drop their ears back on their heads as well, similar to the way in which some dogs show fear or anger. Moose often signal with a combination of these behaviors.

Besides predators, drownings, and traffic accidents, moose face a variety of other hazards. Moose and train collisions are a concern in parts of Alaska and other locales where excessive snow depths make cleared railroad beds inviting for moose to use as a path. When a train comes along a moose has trouble escaping into the deep snowbanks on either side.

Disease and pestilence also take a toll on moose. Killers include the so-called brainworm or moose sickness, a chronic syndrome called wasting disease, and a lungworm that leads to emphysema. Tick infestations also sometimes play a role in depleting the health and resistance of moose.

Moose that live in regions outside the range of white-tailed deer, such as this Alaskan bull, escape the threat of the "brainworm" spread by these deer.

The brainworm may be the most serious health hazard moose face in regions where their range overlaps with that of the parasite's carrier, the white-tailed deer. While *Parelaphostrongylus tenuis* doesn't affect deer, it usually proves fatal to infected moose, who ingest this parasitic roundworm when deer droppings allow it to invade small snails that moose ingest as they eat forest vegetation. Seriously affected moose lose their fear of hazards, including humans, wander onto roads and even into city areas as the brainworm attacks their nervous systems, and eventually succumb to paralysis and inability to function.

Surprisingly enough, the most ragged-looking of moose that one sees in early to mid-spring are usually quite healthy. Moose shed the heavy guard hairs that serve them as winter coats every year. Moose take on a patchwork appearance starting about April, and some wide areas of their flanks and backs appear completely bald by May. They grow a new coat each spring and by early July look much more photogenic.

Late spring and early summer are also the prime seasons for the nuisance insects of the north woods: blackflies, mosquitoes, and deerflies. Because swarms of flies often plague moose, some people theorize that they take refuge in ponds. This escape doesn't work very well, as you often see a cloud of flies hovering over the spot where a moose submerged to feed, waiting to attack when it surfaces.

That moose are sometimes bothered by flies is beyond doubt, but it's more

likely that they come to the ponds to feed. Despite the nuisance presented by these biting insects, they do not appear to take a physical toll on moose, but probably do take a mental toll on them, just as they do on humans who brave their bites to enjoy the thrill of moose watching at this time of year.

Moose watching has become a major recreational pursuit for many folks in recent years. People vacation at Algonquin Provincial Park in Ontario, Baxter State Park and the Moosehead Lake region in Maine, Denali National Park and Kenai National Wildlife Refuge in Alaska, Gaspésie Provincial Park in Quebec, and Grand Teton National Park in Wyoming, as well as at other such places in moose country, just to see these largest deer in the world in their natural habitat. The revenues to moose country businesses related to moose watching are significant.

When added to the money spent in the consumptive pursuit of moose, the total gross value of all moose recreation across North America has been estimated to be hundreds of millions of U.S. dollars annually. Perhaps that's reason enough for us to maintain vigilance to ensure that moose always inhabit our northern forest.

This Wyoming bull lives at one of the many moose watching hot spots in North America—Grand Teton National Park.

SIX

MOOSE FOREVER?

This moose mother ran her twin calves for miles, first down a

paved road and then up a dry streambed, to elude a following grizzly bear.

The moose cow is wearing a radio collar.

The wolves of the

East Fork pack

worked as a team to

bring down the two

moose calves despite

the best efforts of

their mother.

The wolves pulled the first moose calf down at 6:56 P.M. Its sibling fell two minutes later. Mother moose ran back and forth in a desperate attempt to protect her doomed twins, but it was already too late.

Her frantic efforts to chase off the four wolves caught our attention as we drove past the East Fork River in Denali National Park that warm Alaskan spring evening. We set up cameras with long lenses to reach across the thousand feet or so of the riverbed to the scene and watched in awe while we photographed the natural drama that played out before us.

It didn't occur to me then—in fact it didn't occur to me at all—that what I had photographed was more than a rarely seen sight, but also one with historic significance. It was only after we described the scene to a graduate student researching bear activity in Denali several days later that it hit me, when he remarked how exciting it must have been to witness interaction between a moose and descendants of the legendary East Fork wolf pack.

The famed naturalist Adolph Murie studied the East Fork wolf pack intensively from 1939 to 1941. In 1940, he lived in a cabin that I could see as I photographed the futile struggle of that aroused mother moose against an East Fork wolf pack of fifty-seven years later.

Murie never witnessed wolves attacking a moose during that study. But as he wrote in his classic *The Wolves of Mount McKinley*: "Granting that adult moose are difficult prey for wolves, one might suspect that young calves would

be quite susceptible to wolf attack. However, a cow with a calf is a formidable creature and if molested by wolves would probably put up a vigorous fight to protect her young."

Murie was right. The cow fought the wolves for thirty long minutes. Sometimes she would charge the wolves, only to be chased away by one or two. When she chased a wolf, it would cleverly draw her away from her fallen calves so that its comrades could work on their carcasses.

Once the cow moose slipped on the treacherous loose rock of the wide river bar of the East Fork. The wolves united to chase her. They knew that if she fell their meal that day would be a long one.

Why did this moose bring her recently born calves out into the open on that wide river bar where they would be so vulnerable? Was she feeding in the willows along the edge of one of the glacial flows of the river and didn't see the wolves, which blend so well with the gray rock of the bar? Perhaps the wolves chased the moose family out onto that loose rock. Did they know that they would enjoy a better chance to separate her from one of her offspring there?

A healthy adult moose can defend itself quite well with its hoofs. A mother moose could easily ward off the attack of a single wolf, perhaps two, maybe even three.

She may even be able to defend her calf against the attack of a grizzly bear. Adolph Murie described the success of a number of moose, including those

A mother moose will even defend against the attack of a grizzly bear.

defending calves, against grizzlies in his companion work, *The Grizzlies of Mount McKinley.* He also documented the effectiveness of the powerful slashing hoofs of a moose. From field observations of twenty-five summers at Denali National Park, Murie concluded that a cow moose "can and will protect her young against bear attack, at least if the bear is not too big."

Wildlife researchers have documented that black bears, grizzly or brown bears, wolves, and even cougars can and do prey successfully on moose.

Who gets the most moose? Some researchers believe that the most numerous predator species in any ecosystem is responsible for the most predation on any given prey species. The availability of other species as food sources also makes a difference in the impact any predator has on any given prey species.

But are such predators truly enemies of moose? Some wildlife researchers suggest that predators strengthen prey populations by weeding out the sick, genetically inferior, or old and infirm animals. Others believe that predators help prey species by limiting their numbers, thus helping to maintain better balance with the carrying capacity for a given ecosystem. Many other factors, including winter weather, snow depth and ice coating, hunting, poaching, disease, and parasites, also impact on any given population of a species.

Among the predators, black bears have the greatest opportunity to affect moose populations. Black bears share much of the same territory across the moose range, being the most widespread of the most capable moose predators surviving in North America today. While one research project completed on the Kenai Peninsula in Alaska found that black bears caused nearly 60 percent of the mortality of radio-collared moose calves in the study, black bears have apparently had minimal impact on an expanding moose population there or elsewhere. Consider that in Maine, where some twenty thousand black bears coexist with at least thirty thousand moose, black bear predation of moose calves has had minimal impact.

It is also doubtful that a self-respecting black bear would challenge a healthy adult moose. In fact, researchers have found that while brown bears can be an important predator of adult moose, their smaller relatives probably are not.

When given the opportunity, brown bears can take their share of moose calves. Victor Van Ballenberghe's research at Denali National Park in Alaska since 1980 has discovered that moose calves in the study area have experienced very low survival rates in the past seventeen years. Moose calf mortality has averaged between 80 and 90 percent, mostly due to predation by brown bears, the most successful of the three predators in the locale, which wolves and black bears also inhabit.

Such research seems to support what Murie documented from his field observations: that a mother moose can defend against smaller bears, but that she may meet an unequal task in protecting her young against a "full-sized grizzly."

But are bears the most effective predators of moose? Probably not. While

A healthy moose calf represents the future of its species.

OPPOSITE PAGE: By its first fall a calf takes on a much more mooselike appearance. But it still has much to learn from its mother, and needs her protection if it is to become an adult.

both brown and black bears will take advantage of an opportunity to enjoy a meal of a moose calf, and a large brown bear could present a challenge to even a healthy adult moose, both species actually eat mostly nuts, berries, insects, forbs, roots, and grasses.

The studies of a number of researchers indicate that wolves may be the most effective predators of moose. And wolves successfully prey not only on the calves and the infirm, but sometimes also on healthy adult moose.

The interaction of wolves and moose on Isle Royale in Lake Superior has provided much information over the past fifty years. Studies at Isle Royale indicate that the wolf can significantly impact a moose population.

That's not necessarily such a bad thing: in the absence of any predators, the moose population of Isle Royale grew to a number in the late 1920s that exceeded the carrying capacity of the island. When a severe winter struck in 1933–34, hundreds of moose starved to death.

After wolves found their way to Isle Royale over the frozen surface of Lake Superior during the 1940s, many years of interaction between the two species suggested that they might control each other's numbers in some sort of give-and-take. Wolf and moose numbers seemed to achieve a "natural balance" at times.

But the concept that an effective predator such as the wolf maintains a balance with its prey still remains in question. The wolf population of Isle Royale crashed due to an outbreak of canine parvovirus in the early 1980s, and with less predation, the moose population grew to at least 2,400 by 1995. When a severe winter with lots of early and deep snows hit in 1995–96, the moose of Isle Royale once again starved to death in staggering numbers. When researchers counted moose from the air in February 1997, they found only 500 survivors.

A study of cougar predation on moose conducted in Alberta recently revealed that cougars can also be effective killers of calves and yearling moose. The male mountain lions studied actually specialized on moose for the bulk of their diet.

So many factors influence the success rate of any predator within a given ecosystem that wildlife researchers sometimes disagree about their effect on moose. What we do know for sure is that bears, wolves, and cougars, perhaps sometimes even lynx, wolverines, and coyotes, prey on moose as they each play their own role in the natural world.

But moose are not helpless against them. As we have seen, moose have several good defenses. First, they have both an excellent sense of smell and an acute sense of hearing. Both aid them in detecting the presence of a potential threat. A moose will probably avoid any predator that it discovers first.

A cow moose that I photographed as she ran her twins down a paved

By its second summer a moose must know how to fend for itself. This yearling bull will someday grow a fine rack of antlers if it survives.

stretch of Denali National Park's access road was evading a grizzly bear that emerged from the taiga a few minutes later. After a mile or so she took to a dry stream bed and followed it out of sight as her two calves tagged along right behind her.

The bear lost scent of the moose family as soon as it stepped onto the pavement. Did the moose know that she could lose the bear that way? Or did a paved road simply present an easy surface on which to escape? With the adeptness at which moose run across most any terrain, it seems unlikely that

she needed the road to make an escape, especially when you consider that she had to weave around cars and buses.

The powerful front legs of a moose can deliver a skull crusher of a kick. A moose could kill even a large bear with a well-placed kick. Its hind legs are also effective weapons. And a bull moose might even succeed in goring a predator with his antlers in the fall.

Through a combination of its senses and defenses, an adult moose can often avoid or protect itself from most predators. But can a cow moose save

As fall comes again the yearling bull, feeling the forces of its first sexual desires, made a mistake when it approached a mature cow.

her calves from four wolves working together who enjoy a terrain advantage? This one couldn't.

As sad as it is to witness such a tragedy for a moose family, those who respect the natural world must understand that wolves also have a right to survive by making use of the resource—even when that resource happens to be two cute little moose calves.

We have already seen that man is the most effective predator of moose. We humans have in our power the ability to cause the demise of most any species on this earth, and in the case of the moose, we were well on our way toward that at the beginning of the twentieth century. Fortunately, we have learned to control the impulse to kill these magnificent creatures within systems of law and carefully managed hunting seasons that allow for the species to survive.

But human impacts on moose include far more than our ability to hunt them for food or clothing. In the modern world we have a greater ability to impact moose with pollution and the alteration of their natural habitat. One can only hope as we enter the twenty-first century that we remember the past and plan more wisely for the future.

Why is that important? Most people reading this book probably never ate moose meat or wore moosehide clothing. Most probably never will. Certainly most will never need to rely on moose for sustenance. So why do we need moose?

When she worked as a biologist for the United States Fish and Wildlife Service, Rachel Carson, whom many credit as the founder of modern environmentalism, wrote that "All the people of a country have a direct interest in conservation."

She went on to describe the many ways that humans enjoy natural resources, either by hunting, fishing, through study and observation, by photographing nature, or simply in the contemplation of the forms, shapes, and colors found in the natural world. And then she concluded: "But for all people, the preservation of wildlife and of wildlife habitat means also the preservation of the basic resources of the earth, which men, as well as animals, must have in order to live."

Would we survive if moose no longer roamed our northern forest? If it were just the moose that no longer existed, surely. But after the moose were gone, what next? The bears and the wolves that include them in their diet? And then what?

I only know for sure that if moose vanished from the earth it would be a far less exciting planet on which to live. Why? Because moose are somehow very special.

Maybe it's because they're often such gentle animals, for all of their size and bulk. Thoreau was right: moose can be just "great frightened rabbits." But they can also be such powerful and unpredictable animals. Moose truly can

Now a bull in his prime, this handsome moose makes one hope that we will enjoy moose forever.

be one of the major forces to behold in the animal world.

But wait. I am prejudiced: I've been in love with moose ever since seeing my first one as a youngster. In recent years, that love of moose has led to the pursuit of them with a camera all across North America, to places as diverse as the Gaspé Peninsula of Quebec, to the Kenai Peninsula and Denali National Park in Alaska, to Elk Island National Park in Alberta, all over the Maine woods and to British Columbia. I've photographed hundreds of moose and have over ten thousand pictures of them.

And after all of that, I'm still in love with moose. Maybe if I relate one last moose story you'll understand why.

It was the third week of August as we clustered along the road at Sable Pass in Denali National Park. The group of professional wildlife photographers waited for one of several monster bull moose feeding in a ravine several hundred yards off the road to come close enough to get a telling image. The lands on both sides of the road for the five miles of Sable Pass are closed to people, as they're reserved for the wildlife only.

We'd seen these four big bulls, their massive racks seemingly about to burst out of velvet, just beyond effective camera range on one side of the road or the other every time we drove through Sable Pass. If we could only be there when they crossed!

When we'd see them close enough to the road to encourage it, we would stop and wait, sometimes for hours, in the hope that they might at least come a bit closer, perhaps even cross the road. And so we'd wait as the bulls browsed and slept and browsed again, teasing us with their proximity that was literally so near and yet so far, even for the powerful telephoto lenses we'd set up on our tripods.

And then one day one of the big bulls decided that he was going to cross the road while we stood there.

The band of photographers fanned out as they saw him prancing up and

I got one quick photograph as the monster bull studied the other photographers, and then he was gone.

down in the ravine as he made ready to cross. You couldn't tell where he'd make his crossing; he probably didn't know himself.

Suddenly he pivoted toward the road and began to run. He loomed larger and larger in the viewfinder and I suddenly realized that he was going to cross right where I stood! I took a last shot before snatching up my tripod and ran to get out of his way.

The monster moose slowed at the roadside and stepped effortlessly onto the gravel surface. He paused only one hundred feet away and turned to look at me. That moose towered over my head! He had the widest rack of antlers I'd ever seen and he must have weighed at least 1,500 pounds.

There are no trees to climb at Sable Pass, and with the truck way up the road, I would have been in grave danger if the bull had decided to charge. He could easily have run me down. He could have killed me with a single kick.

But he just looked at me in that special way that moose do when they're not angry or scared. I didn't have the chance to capture the look before he turned to observe the other photographers who stood farther up the road, but I'll always remember it. It seemed almost that when our eyes met his said: Thanks for getting out of my way.

I did get a quick shot of him as he watched the other photographers. And then he was gone.

SELECTED BIBLIOGRAPHY

Ballard, Warren, and Vince Crichton, ed. *The Moose Call*. Winnipeg, MN: *Journal Alces*. Selected articles from Volumes 1–5: December 1994, September 1995, June 1996, December 1996 and June 1997.

Ballard, Warren, and Victor van Ballenberghe. "Limitation and Regulation of Moose Populations: The Role of Predation." *Canadian Journal of Zoology*, 1994.

Buss, M.E., and Timmerman, H.R. "The Status and Management of Moose in North America. Thunder Bay, ON: *Alces Journal* 31, 1995.

Dunn, Francis et al. *Moose Management Plan*. Augusta, ME: Maine Department of Inland Fisheries and Game, 1975.

Fenton, Mildred Adams, and Carroll Lane. *The Fossil Book*. New York: Doubleday, 1958.

Geist, Valerius. "Moose: Genus Alces." In *Grzimek's Encyclopedia of Mammals, Volume 5*. New York: McGraw-Hill, 1990.

Kay, Charles E. "Aboriginal Overkill and the Biogeography of Moose in Western North America." Thunder Bay, ON: *Alces Journal* 33, 1997.

Miquelle, Dale G., and Victor van Ballenberghe. "Rutting Behavior of Moose in Central Alaska." Thunder Bay, ON: *Alces Journal* 32, 1996.

Murie, Adolph. *The Grizzlies of Mount McKinley*. Seattle, WA: University of Washington Press, 1985.

_____. *The Wolves of Mount McKinley*. Seattle, WA: University of Washinton Press, 1985.

Peterson, Randolph L. *North American Moose*. Toronto: University of Toronto Press, 1955.

Seton, Ernest Thompson. *Lives of Game Animals, Volume III*. New York: Doubleday, Doran and Co., 1927.

Silliker, Bill, Jr. *Maine Moose Watcher's Guide*. Berwick: ME: R.L. Lemke Co., 1993.

INDEX